# Menton France Travel Guide 2025

*An Exploration of the French Riviera Gem with Local Tips on Where to Stay, What to See, and How to Experience It All*

Bryan J. Zehner

*Disclaimer:* The information, contacts, websites, and costs provided in this book were accurate at the time of publication. Readers are advised to verify current details as information may have changed since publication.

# Content

# Introduction to Menton

Menton is a picturesque town located on the French Riviera, nestled between the Mediterranean Sea and the rugged foothills of the Alps. It lies near the border with Italy, just a short distance from the bustling city of Nice and the glamorous city-state of Monaco. Known for its mild climate, stunning natural beauty, and charming old town, Menton is often referred to as the "Pearl of France."

The town's geography contributes to its unique climate, characterized by mild winters and warm summers. The combination of sea breezes and the protection offered by surrounding hills creates an ideal environment for cultivating a variety of plants, including the famous Menton lemons. The town's architecture reflects its rich history, with colorful buildings and narrow streets that evoke a sense of timelessness and charm.

Menton's location offers a blend of beautiful landscapes and cultural heritage. Its coastal setting provides stunning views of the Mediterranean Sea, while its proximity to the Alps offers a dramatic backdrop. The town's position on the French-Italian border enhances its cultural diversity, with influences evident in its cuisine, architecture, and traditions.

Menton has a rich history that dates back to Roman times. Originally a fishing village, it became an important trading post during the Middle Ages. The town's strategic location on the Mediterranean coast made it a valuable asset for various powers over the centuries. It was part of the County of Savoy until 1848 when it was ceded to France.

In the 19th century, Menton emerged as a popular destination for European aristocrats and wealthy travelers seeking respite from the colder climates of their home countries. Its mild climate and scenic beauty made it an attractive destination for those seeking health benefits, and it quickly gained a reputation as a resort town. The influence of these early visitors is still evident today in the town's architecture and cultural institutions.

Menton's cultural heritage is also reflected in its festivals and events. The Lemon Festival (Fête du Citron), held annually in February, is a major highlight, celebrating the town's citrus production with elaborate floats and displays made entirely of lemons and oranges. The town's vibrant cultural scene includes music festivals, art exhibitions, and historical reenactments that showcase its diverse heritage.

Menton offers a unique combination of natural beauty, historical charm, and cultural richness, making it an attractive destination for a wide range of travelers. Its mild climate is a major draw, providing a pleasant experience year-round. The town's stunning coastal views, lush gardens, and historical architecture create a picturesque setting that appeals to those seeking both relaxation and exploration.

Visitors to Menton can enjoy a variety of outdoor activities, from lounging on its beautiful beaches to exploring the surrounding hills and countryside. The town's gardens, such as the Serre de la Madone and the Jardin Botanique Exotique, offer serene environments for leisurely strolls and are home to a diverse collection of plant species.

Cultural enthusiasts will find much to appreciate in Menton's museums, art galleries, and historical sites. The town's rich history and artistic heritage are preserved in its well-maintained architecture and cultural institutions. Additionally, the vibrant local festivals and events provide opportunities to experience the town's lively traditions and community spirit.

For food lovers, Menton offers a delightful culinary experience with its array of restaurants and cafés serving both local and international cuisine. The town's markets and food festivals allow visitors to sample regional specialties, including its renowned lemons.

### Best Time to Visit Menton

*Spring (March to May):* Spring is an excellent time to visit Menton, as the weather is pleasant with temperatures ranging from 15°C to 22°C (59°F to 72°F). The town's gardens and parks are in full bloom, and outdoor activities are enjoyable. Spring is also when the town begins to prepare for its famous Lemon Festival, providing an opportunity to experience local culture and festivities.

*Summer (June to August):* Summer in Menton is warm, with temperatures typically ranging from 20°C to 30°C (68°F to 86°F). This is the peak tourist season, and the town's beaches and outdoor attractions are bustling with visitors. Summer is ideal for beachgoers and those who enjoy vibrant nightlife and cultural events. However, it is also the most crowded time of the year, so travelers should plan and book accommodations in advance.

*Autumn (September to November):* Autumn is a wonderful time to visit Menton, as the weather remains warm with temperatures ranging from 15°C to 25°C (59°F to 77°F). The summer crowds have diminished, and visitors can enjoy a more relaxed atmosphere. The town's festivals and markets continue into the fall, providing a chance to experience local traditions and seasonal produce.

*Winter (December to February):* Winter in Menton is mild compared to other regions, with temperatures ranging from 8°C to 15°C (46°F to 59°F). This is a quieter time to visit, and while it may not be ideal for beach activities, it is perfect for exploring the town's cultural sites and enjoying the serene atmosphere. The winter months also feature the Lemon Festival, a highlight for many visitors.

*Menton offers a range of experiences throughout the year. The best time to visit depends on personal preferences and the type of activities one wishes to enjoy. Each season brings its own unique charm to this beautiful town.*

# Chapter 1

## *Getting to Menton*

### Transportation Options (Train, Bus, Car)

Traveling to Menton from nearby cities or countries is straightforward and offers several options depending on your preferences and budget.

### *Train*

One of the most convenient and scenic ways to reach Menton is by train. The town is well-connected through the French railway network, making it easily accessible from major cities such as Nice, Paris, and even international locations.

The train journey from Nice to Menton takes approximately 30 minutes, with frequent departures throughout the day. The trains are operated by SNCF, France's national railway company, and offer comfortable and efficient travel. Passengers can enjoy beautiful views of the Mediterranean coastline along the way.

For those traveling from Paris, direct trains to Nice are available, from which travelers can transfer to a regional train heading to Menton. Tickets for this route can be purchased through the SNCF website (www.sncf.com), where schedules and prices are also available. A one-way ticket from Nice to Menton typically costs around €5.30, though this can vary based on the time of day and how far in advance the tickets are booked.

### *Bus*

Another economical choice for reaching Menton is by bus. The Lignes d'Azur bus service, particularly bus number 100, provides a direct route from Nice to Menton. This journey takes about 1.5 hours and is a budget-friendly option, with a fare of approximately €1.50.

The buses depart from Nice's Port area, which is easily reachable from various parts of the city. While the bus ride can be longer due to multiple stops and potential traffic, it offers a cost-effective way to travel. Tickets can be purchased at kiosks, directly on the bus, or through the Lignes d'Azur website (www.lignesdazur.com). It is wise to check the schedule ahead of time to plan the journey effectively.

*Car*

Driving to Menton provides flexibility and the opportunity to explore the surrounding areas at your own pace. The drive from Nice to Menton usually takes around 45 minutes, depending on traffic. The route follows the A8 motorway, which connects major cities along the French Riviera.

Upon arriving in Menton, parking is available in various locations, including public parking lots and street parking. It is advisable to check parking regulations and availability, especially during peak tourist seasons. Travelers can use navigation systems or maps to plan their route, and car rental services are available in Nice for those who prefer to drive. A valid driver's license and awareness of local driving regulations are essential.

## Tips for Arriving at Nice Airport

Nice Côte d'Azur Airport (NCE) serves as the main gateway for international travelers heading to Menton. The airport is situated approximately 30 kilometers (18 miles) from Menton, making it a convenient entry point.

Upon arrival, passengers will go through customs and immigration checks, so it is important to have all necessary travel documents, including passports and visas, readily available. After clearing customs, travelers can proceed to the baggage claim area to collect any checked luggage.

Nice Côte d'Azur Airport offers a range of facilities, including information desks, currency exchange, and car rental services, which can be useful for arriving passengers.

To travel from the airport to Menton, several options are available. One of the most efficient ways is to take the train. The airport is connected to Nice's central train station (Gare de Nice-Ville) by the Airport Express (Bus 99), which provides a convenient transfer. From the train station, regional trains to Menton are frequent and provide a scenic journey. The entire trip from the airport to Menton by train takes about an hour.

Alternatively, direct buses from the airport to Nice's central bus station are also available, from which travelers can catch the Lignes d'Azur bus to Menton. For those who prefer a more direct route, taxis are available at the airport and typically take about 45 minutes to reach Menton, with fares ranging from €70 to €90.

Another option is car rental, which is offered by a number of significant businesses at Nice Airport. The terminal building houses the car rental desks. Having a car rental gives you freedom and the chance to see the area at your own speed.

**Local Transport in Menton (Buses, Taxis)**

Once in Menton, the local transportation system is designed to facilitate travel within the town and to nearby areas.

Menton's local bus network is managed by the "Réseau des Transports de la Communauté d'Agglomération du Pays Mentonnais" (TPCM). The buses cover a range of routes that connect the town's main attractions, neighborhoods, and surrounding areas. Local bus services are frequent, and schedules can be accessed on the TPCM website (www.tpcm.fr).

The cost of a single bus ticket is around €1.50, though there are options for multi-ride passes and day tickets for those who plan to use the bus frequently. Bus stops are clearly marked, and schedules are posted at each stop, making it easy to plan your travels.

Taxis are also readily available in Menton, offering a convenient way to get around the town. Taxi stands are located at key points, such as the train station and major tourist areas. Taxis can be hailed directly or booked in advance by phone. Local taxi services include "Taxis Mentonnais" and "Taxis Riviera," with contact numbers available on their respective websites. Taxi fares are metered, with short trips within Menton typically costing around €10 to €15. Longer journeys or trips to nearby towns may incur higher fares.

**Useful Contacts:**

- **TPCM (Local Bus Services):**
  www.tpcm.fr
- **Taxis Mentonnais:** +33 (0)4 93 35 44 60
- **Taxis Riviera:** +33 (0)4 93 41 03 25

**Flight Options**

For international travelers, Nice Côte d'Azur Airport (NCE) is the main entry point to Menton. The airport offers numerous flight options from various global destinations. It is advisable to check for flights well in advance and compare prices to find the best deals.

Airlines operating at Nice Airport include major international carriers, as well as regional airlines.

Travelers should visit the Nice Côte d'Azur Airport website for the latest information on flight options, including arrivals, departures, and airline contact details. The airport website is a valuable resource for planning your journey and obtaining up-to-date travel information.

**Useful Contacts:**

- **Nice Côte d'Azur Airport:**
  www.nice.aeroport.fr

# Chapter 2

## *Where to Stay*

### Overview of Accommodation Types

Menton, a picturesque town on the French Riviera, offers a diverse range of accommodation options suited to various preferences and budgets. From luxurious hotels to charming guesthouses and unique vacation rentals, each type of lodging provides different experiences and amenities, allowing travelers to find the perfect fit for their stay.

Hotels in Menton cater to a variety of needs, from high-end luxury to more affordable options. Luxury hotels are often situated along the seafront or in central locations, offering amenities such as swimming pools, spas, and fine dining. These establishments typically provide breathtaking views of the Mediterranean Sea and convenient access to local attractions. For those on a tighter budget, mid-range and budget hotels offer comfortable accommodations with essential amenities like Wi-Fi, air conditioning, and breakfast.

Guesthouses, or "chambres d'hôtes," present a more intimate and personalized lodging experience compared to traditional hotels. These smaller, often family-run establishments offer a homely atmosphere and the chance to interact with local hosts. Many guesthouses include breakfast and provide additional features such as garden areas or private terraces, enhancing the overall stay.

Vacation rentals are an excellent choice for those seeking more space and independence. Options include apartments, houses, and villas that can be rented for short or long periods. Vacation rentals are particularly popular with families or groups, providing home-like comforts such as fully equipped kitchens and private outdoor spaces. This type of accommodation allows guests to enjoy a more self-sufficient and personalized stay.

For a unique lodging experience, Menton also offers distinctive options such as stays in converted historic buildings, luxurious villas with private amenities, or eco-friendly accommodations. These special lodgings provide an opportunity to enjoy Menton in a memorable and unique way.

## Recommended Hotels and Guesthouses

**Hotel Royal Westminster** is a premier choice for travelers seeking luxury. Located at 23 Promenade du Soleil, 06500 Menton, France, this four-star hotel is situated directly on the seafront, offering stunning Mediterranean views. The hotel features elegant rooms, an outdoor swimming pool, a fitness center, and a restaurant serving gourmet cuisine. Room rates generally start around €150 per night. For more information or to make a reservation, visit https://www.vacancesbleues.fr or call +33 (0)4 93 35 24 00.

**Best Western Premier Hotel Prince De Galles** is another excellent option, offering a central location at 2 Avenue Felix Faure, 06500 Menton, France. This four-star hotel provides well-appointed rooms, free Wi-Fi, a bar, and a fitness center. The rates for a standard room typically begin at approximately €130 per night. For reservations and additional details, visit https://www.bestwestern.com or call +33 (0)4 93 35 21 03.

**Hotel Napoléon** is situated at 9 Avenue Boyer, 06500 Menton, France, and offers a more affordable stay while maintaining comfort. This three-star hotel features cozy rooms, a garden area, and a breakfast buffet. Room rates for this centrally located hotel generally start at €100 per night. For more information or to book, visit https://www.hotel-napoleon-menton.com or contact +33 (0)4 93 35 80 12.

**Le Hameau** is a charming guesthouse located at 31 Avenue de la Madone, 06500 Menton, France. It provides a personal and homely atmosphere with beautifully furnished rooms, a garden, and a communal lounge area. Breakfast is included, featuring fresh local produce. The starting price for a room is about €90 per night. For reservations and additional information, visit https://www.le hameau-menton.com or call +33 (0)4 93 35 66 77.

**La Maison d'Hôtes** offers a cozy and welcoming environment at 16 Rue de la République, 06500 Menton, France. This guesthouse features tastefully decorated rooms, a lovely terrace, and a hearty breakfast service. Room rates typically start at €85 per night. For more details or to make a reservation, visit https://www.lamaisondhotes-menton.com or contact +33 (0)4 93 35 45 78.

**Vacation Rentals and Unique Stays**

**Apartment Le Soleil** provides a spacious and modern rental option at 4 Boulevard de Garavan, 06500 Menton, France. This apartment includes two bedrooms, a fully equipped kitchen, and a private balcony with stunning sea views. Ideal for families or groups, it is available for around €1,000 per week. For availability and bookings, visit https://www.apartment soleil-menton.com or contact the owner at +33 (0)4 93 35 55 44.

**Villa Belle Vue** offers a luxurious stay with amenities such as a private pool, garden, and outdoor dining area. Located at 15 Rue des Acacias, 06500 Menton, France, this villa features four bedrooms and high-end facilities, making it perfect for larger groups or families. Weekly rental rates start at approximately €3,000. For more information or to book this property, visit https://www.villabellevue-menton.com or call +33 (0)4 93 35 66 88.

**Château de Menton** provides a unique lodging experience in a historic setting at 5 Rue du Château, 06500 Menton, France. This property, housed in a beautifully restored château, features elegant rooms, a large garden, and an on-site restaurant. Room rates start around €200 per night. For reservations and additional details, visit https://www.chateaudementon.com or call +33 (0)4 93 35 77 99.

**Eco-Lodge Les Oliviers** emphasizes sustainable practices and offers an eco-friendly accommodation option at 23 Avenue des

Mimosas, 06500 Menton, France. The lodge provides comfortable lodgings with picturesque views, promoting environmental conservation. Rates typically start at €120 per night. For more details or to make a reservation, visit https://www.ecolodgelesoliviers.com or contact +33 (0)4 93 35 88 66.

Choosing the right accommodation in Menton will enhance your travel experience, whether you prefer luxury, a homely touch, or a unique stay. With a range of options available, you can find the perfect place to stay and enjoy all that this beautiful French Riviera destination has to offer.

# Chapter 3

## *Top Attractions*

### Jardins Serre de la Madone

Jardins Serre de la Madone, located at 74 Route de Gorbio, 06500 Menton, is a botanical garden renowned for its rich collection of exotic plants and serene landscapes. This garden, designed by the French horticulturist Lawrence Johnston in the early 20th century, spans approximately 7 hectares and offers a tranquil retreat into nature.

The garden's design integrates a variety of themes, including Mediterranean, tropical, and subtropical flora. Visitors can explore lush, landscaped areas featuring rare plants, vibrant flower beds, and scenic water features. The gardens are divided into distinct sections, each showcasing different plant species and horticultural styles, reflecting Johnston's extensive travels and botanical expertise.

Admission to Jardins Serre de la Madone costs around €6 for adults, with reduced rates available for seniors and children. The garden is open to the public from March to November, with specific opening hours that vary by season.

Nearby accommodation options include the **Hôtel Menton Riviera**, located at 1 Avenue de la Gare, 06500 Menton. This three-star hotel offers comfortable rooms and convenient access to local attractions. Room rates at Hôtel Menton Riviera start at approximately €85 per night. For reservations or more information, visit https://www.hotelmentonriviera.com or call +33 (0)4 93 35 10 45.

*hotelmentonriviera@orange.fr*

To reach Jardins Serre de la Madone, visitors can take public transportation or drive. The garden is accessible via bus routes from the Menton train station. For those driving, parking is available on-site. The location is approximately a 10-minute drive from the center of Menton.

## Menton Old Town (Vieux Menton)

Menton Old Town, or Vieux Menton, is the historical heart of the town, characterized by its narrow, winding streets and colorful facades. This charming area is located along the coast and provides a picturesque setting with its Mediterranean architecture and historic buildings.

Walking through Vieux Menton offers an immersive experience into the town's history and culture. The old town features a blend of traditional houses, bustling markets, and quaint shops. Visitors can explore notable sites such as the Place du Cap, a lively square surrounded by cafes and restaurants, and the Rue Pietonne, a pedestrian street lined with boutiques and artisanal shops.

A key highlight of Vieux Menton is the **Place des Marchés**, an open-air market where visitors can purchase local produce, flowers, and crafts. The market is open daily except Mondays, with vendors setting up their stalls in the morning hours.

Nearby, the **Hôtel Napoléon** at 9 Avenue Boyer, 06500 Menton, provides comfortable lodging with easy access to the Old Town. Room rates start at around €100 per night. For more call +33 (0)4 93 35 80 12.

To explore Menton Old Town, visitors can arrive by train to Menton station and then walk or take a short taxi ride to the historic area. The town center is well-connected by local buses and taxis, making it easy to navigate and enjoy the various attractions.

## Basilica of Saint-Michael the Archangel

The Basilica of Saint-Michael the Archangel, located at Place du Palais de Justice, 06500 Menton, is a significant religious and architectural landmark in Menton. This Baroque-style church, constructed between 1619 and 1639, is renowned for its elaborate facade and richly decorated interior.

The basilica's exterior features intricate stucco work and a striking bell tower, while the interior boasts ornate altars, detailed frescoes, and grandiose chandeliers. The church is dedicated to Saint Michael, the patron saint of Menton, and serves as a place of worship and historical interest.

Admission to the basilica is free, though donations are appreciated. The church is open to visitors daily, with specific hours that can be verified by contacting the parish office. For the most current information call +33 (0)4 93 35 83 54.

The **Hotel Royal Westminster**, located at 23 Promenade du Soleil, 06500 Menton, is situated close to the basilica and offers luxurious accommodations with beautiful sea views. Room rates start at approximately €150 per night. For reservations and more details call +33 (0)4 93 35 24 00.

The basilica is easily accessible from the center of Menton. Visitors can take a short walk from the town center or use local public transportation options. The church is centrally located, making it convenient to include in a day's itinerary of exploring Menton.

# Menton Museum of Art and History

The Menton Museum of Art and History, situated at 2 Rue de la Conception, 06500 Menton, offers a comprehensive look at the region's rich cultural heritage. This museum features a diverse collection of art and historical artifacts, highlighting Menton's evolution from antiquity to the present.

The museum's exhibits include archaeological finds, period costumes, and works by local artists. Key displays feature items related to the town's history, such as Roman artifacts and artworks from the 19th and 20th centuries. The museum also hosts temporary exhibitions that cover various themes related to art and history.

Admission to the Menton Museum of Art and History is approximately €5 for adults, with discounts available for seniors and children. The museum is open from Tuesday to Sunday, with specific hours that may vary. For the latest information on opening times and exhibitions call +33 (0)4 93 35 82 11.

Nearby lodging options include the **Best Western Premier Hotel Prince De Galles**, located at 2 Avenue Felix Faure, 06500 Menton. This hotel provides upscale accommodations and is within walking distance of the museum. Room rates typically start at around €130 per night. For more information or to book a stay call +33 (0)4 93 35 21 03.

Visitors can reach the museum easily from various parts of Menton. The museum is centrally located, and walking from nearby hotels or public transportation stops is straightforward. Local buses and taxis also provide convenient access to the museum's location.

# Chapter 4

## *Things to Do*

### Beaches and Coastal Activities

Menton, located on the French Riviera, is renowned for its stunning beaches and array of coastal activities. The town's Mediterranean climate and scenic coastline make it a prime destination for beachgoers and those seeking aquatic recreation.

One of the most popular beaches in Menton is **Plage des Sablettes**, located along Boulevard de

Garavan. This beach features fine sand, clear waters, and a relaxed atmosphere. It is ideal for sunbathing, swimming, and enjoying the picturesque sea views. The beach is equipped with amenities such as sunbeds, umbrellas, and beachside restaurants. Admission to the beach is free, though some private sections may charge for access to loungers and other services. Expect to pay around €15-€30 per day for a set of two sunbeds and an umbrella.

Nearby, the **Hôtel Napoléon** at 9 Avenue Boyer, 06500 Menton, offers convenient accommodation with easy access to Plage des Sablettes. Room rates start at approximately €100 per night. For reservations or more information call +33 (0)4 93 35 80 12.

For those interested in more active coastal pursuits, **Plage du Casino** is another excellent option. Located at 2 Avenue de la Gare, this beach provides opportunities for various water sports, including kayaking and paddleboarding. Rental services for equipment are available on-site, and prices typically range from €10-€20 per hour.

To get to the beaches of Menton, visitors can use local public transportation, such as buses and trains, which connect the main town areas to the coastal spots. Walking from central Menton to these beaches is also quite feasible, as many are within a short distance from the town center.

## Hiking and Outdoor Adventures

Menton's surrounding natural landscapes offer excellent opportunities for hiking and outdoor adventures. The region's diverse terrain includes coastal paths, forest trails, and mountainous routes, providing options for hikers of varying skill levels.

One notable hiking destination is the **Montagne du Coq**, situated just outside Menton. This trail offers panoramic views of the Mediterranean Sea and the surrounding landscape. It takes two to three hours to do the moderately difficult hike. The trailhead can be accessed via a short drive from Menton, with parking available at the base of the mountain. It is advisable to bring sturdy hiking shoes, water, and sun protection.

Another popular spot is the **Col de la Madone**, a scenic mountain pass known for its picturesque views and well-maintained trails. The Col de la Madone is accessible by car, with parking available near the trailheads. This area offers various routes, from easy walks to more strenuous hikes, making it suitable for different levels of hiking enthusiasts.

Accommodation options near these hiking trails include the **Hôtel Le Royal Westminster**, located at 23 Promenade du Soleil, 06500 Menton. This hotel offers comfortable rooms and beautiful views, with room rates starting at around €150 per night. For more details or to make a reservation call +33 (0)4 93 35 24 00.

Local hiking clubs and tour operators offer guided hikes and outdoor activities. For more information call +33 (0)4 92 10 05 00.

**Shopping and Local Markets**

Menton boasts a vibrant shopping scene, characterized by its local markets and boutique stores. The town's markets are an excellent way to experience the local culture and find unique products.

The **Marché Couvert de Menton**, located at 7 Avenue de la Gare, is the main covered market in Menton. This market features a variety of stalls selling fresh produce, local cheeses, meats, and baked goods. The market operates daily except Mondays, with opening hours typically from 7:00 AM to 1:00 PM. It is an ideal place to sample local specialties and purchase gourmet items.

For a more traditional market experience, the **Marché des Halles** is held in the town center and offers a wide selection of fruits, vegetables, and artisanal products. This market is open on Wednesdays and Saturdays, providing visitors with an opportunity to explore local flavors and crafts.

In addition to markets, Menton has several shopping districts with boutique stores and luxury shops. The **Rue Piétonne**, a pedestrian street in the heart of Menton, is lined with fashion boutiques, jewelry stores, and souvenir shops. Here, visitors can browse through high-end clothing, accessories, and unique gifts.

Nearby accommodation options include the **Hôtel Menton Riviera**, located at 1 Avenue de la Gare, 06500 Menton. This hotel offers comfortable lodging with easy access to local markets and shopping areas. Room rates start at approximately €85 per night. For reservations or more information, visit https://www.hotelmentonriviera.com or call +33 (0)4 93 35 10 45.

## Cultural Events and Festivals

Menton's cultural scene is rich and diverse, with numerous events and festivals taking place throughout the year. These celebrations offer insights into the town's traditions, arts, and local life.

One of the most prominent events is the **Fête du Citron**, or Lemon Festival, held annually in February. This festival celebrates Menton's famous citrus fruits with elaborate floats, street parades, and themed decorations. The event draws thousands of visitors and features live entertainment, music, and performances. Admission to the festival's main attractions is generally around €10-€15, with various ticket options available for different activities and events.

Another significant event is the **Menton Jazz Festival**, held in the summer months. This festival showcases international and local jazz musicians, offering a series of concerts and performances in various venues across the town. Tickets for the festival's concerts typically range from €20-€50, depending on the performance and venue.

The **Festival des Jardins** is another notable event, taking place in the fall. This festival highlights garden design and horticulture, with exhibitions and workshops held in different gardens and public spaces throughout Menton.

Accommodation options during these festivals include the **Hôtel Napoléon** at 9 Avenue Boyer, 06500 Menton, which offers comfortable lodging with convenient access to festival venues. Room rates start at approximately €100 per night. For reservations or more details call +33 (0)4 93 35 80 12.

# Chapter 5

## *Dining and Nightlife*

### Best Restaurants and Cafés

One of the top dining establishments in Menton is **Le Galion**, located at 8 Rue du Vieux Collège. This restaurant is known for its sophisticated Mediterranean cuisine and elegant ambiance. The menu features a variety of dishes prepared with fresh, local ingredients, including seafood, meats, and seasonal vegetables. Main courses typically range from €25 to €50, depending on the dish. For a reservation or more information, visit https://www.legalion-restaurant.com or call +33 (0)4 93 35 10 03.

Another highly recommended restaurant is **La Belle Époque**, situated at 5 Avenue du Général Leclerc. This establishment offers a refined dining experience with a menu that emphasizes French cuisine and gourmet dishes. The restaurant's décor combines classic elegance with contemporary touches, creating a comfortable and stylish setting. Main courses at La Belle Époque generally cost between €30 and €60. Reservations can be made by calling +33 (0)4 93 35 22 42.

For a more casual dining experience, **Le Bistrot du Port**, located at 2 Quai Bonaparte, provides a relaxed atmosphere and a menu focused on traditional French bistro fare. Popular dishes include steak frites, salads, and seafood platters. Prices for main courses at Le Bistrot du Port are typically between €15 and €30. To learn more call +33 (0)4 93 35 73 62.

**Café des Arts**, at 14 Place d'Armes, is a delightful spot for a light meal or a coffee break. This café offers a range of pastries, sandwiches, and beverages in a charming setting with outdoor seating. The average cost for a meal here is around €10 to €20. +33 (0)4 93 35 19 80.

## Local Specialties and Cuisine

Menton's cuisine reflects its Mediterranean heritage, featuring a variety of fresh ingredients and flavors. The town is renowned for its local specialties, including citrus fruits, seafood, and traditional French dishes.

A notable local specialty is **Mentonnaise Lemon**, which plays a prominent role in many regional dishes. This tangy fruit is used in a range of culinary creations, from lemon tarts and cakes to savory dishes such as lemon-infused fish. Many restaurants, such as Le Galion and La Belle Époque, incorporate this distinctive ingredient into their menus, offering guests a taste of Menton's unique flavor.

Another local favorite is **Pan Bagnat**, a traditional Niçoise sandwich made with a round loaf of bread filled with ingredients such as tuna, olives, tomatoes, and hard-boiled eggs. This flavorful and satisfying sandwich is commonly served at cafés and casual dining spots throughout Menton.

Seafood lovers will appreciate the fresh catch available in Menton. Dishes such as **Bouillabaisse**, a traditional Provençal fish stew, and **Sole Meunière**, a classic French preparation of sole fish, are popular choices. These dishes highlight the region's access to high-quality seafood and are often featured on restaurant menus.

For dessert, **Tarte au Citron** (lemon tart) is a must-try. This sweet and tangy tart, often made with Menton lemons, offers a delightful end to any meal. Many local patisseries and restaurants serve this dessert, allowing visitors to experience the region's citrus flavors in a delicious and traditional form.

Visitors interested in learning more about local cuisine can also explore the **Menton Food Market**, located at 7 Avenue de la Gare. This market features a variety of fresh produce, artisanal products, and local specialties, providing an opportunity to sample and purchase regional foods.

**Nightlife Options and Entertainment**

Menton's nightlife scene offers a range of options for evening entertainment, from lively bars and nightclubs to more relaxed venues for a casual drink. The town's nightlife caters to various preferences, providing something for everyone to enjoy.

**Le Relais des Douanes**, located at 3 Rue Saint-Michel, is a popular bar known for its cozy atmosphere and extensive selection of beverages. The bar features a variety of cocktails, wines, and craft beers, making it a great spot for a night out with friends or a casual drink. The average cost for a drink at Le Relais des Douanes is around €8 to €15.  +33 (0)4 93 35 53 54.

For those interested in dancing and lively entertainment, **Le Club 22**, situated at 22 Avenue de la Gare, offers a vibrant atmosphere with DJ performances and dancing. This nightclub is popular among both locals and visitors, featuring a range of music genres and a lively crowd. Entry fees typically range from €10 to €20, depending on the night and special events. +33 (0)4 93 35 19 90.

For a more relaxed evening, **Le Café de Paris**, located at 1 Place de la Mairie, provides a charming setting for a drink or a light meal. This café offers a range of beverages and light fare, with outdoor seating available for enjoying the evening ambiance. Prices for drinks and snacks at Le Café de Paris generally range from €5 to €15. +33 (0)4 93 35 03 44.

Throughout the year, Menton hosts various cultural and entertainment events, including concerts, theater performances, and festivals. The **Menton Tourist Office** provides information on current and upcoming events, allowing visitors to plan their evenings according to their interests. +33 (0)4 92 10 05 00.

## 10-Day Itinerary for Exploring Menton and the French Riviera

### Day 1: Arrival in Menton

- **Morning**: Arrive at Nice Côte d'Azur Airport. Take a train or bus to Menton. Check in at your accommodation.
- **Afternoon**: Stroll along the Promenade du Soleil to get acquainted with the town. Relax at a café and enjoy a light lunch.
- **Evening**: Dinner at a local restaurant. Explore the nearby Old Town (Vieux Menton) and enjoy a leisurely evening.

**Day 2: Discover Menton's Gardens**

- **Morning**: Visit the Jardins Serre de la Madone. Explore the beautifully landscaped gardens.
- **Afternoon**: Have lunch at a nearby café. Continue to the Jardin botanique exotique

de Menton for a look at exotic plant species.

- **Evening**: Dinner at a restaurant in the Old Town.


## Day 3: Cultural and Historical Exploration

- **Morning**: Visit the Basilica of Saint-Michael the Archangel. Explore the historical architecture and interiors.
- **Afternoon**: Lunch at a nearby restaurant. Visit the Menton Museum of Art and History to learn about the region's past.
- **Evening**: Enjoy dinner at a local bistro. Experience Menton's nightlife at a local bar or café.

### Day 4: Beach Day and Coastal Relaxation

- **Morning**: Spend the morning at the Plage des Sablettes or another local beach. Enjoy sunbathing and swimming.
- **Afternoon**: Have a beachside lunch. Try water sports like paddle boarding or kayaking.
- **Evening**: Dinner at a seaside restaurant. Take a sunset stroll along the beach.

### Day 5: Day Trip to Roquebrune-Cap-Martin

- **Morning**: Take a bus or drive to Roquebrune-Cap-Martin. Visit the medieval Roquebrune Castle.
- **Afternoon**: Lunch in Roquebrune-Cap-Martin. Explore the

Cap-Martin area and enjoy its coastal views.

- **Evening**: Return to Menton. Have dinner at a neighborhood eatery and unwind afterward.

## Day 6: Excursion to Monaco

- **Morning**: Take a train or bus to Monaco. See the Monaco Cathedral and the Prince's Palace.
- **Afternoon**: Lunch in Monaco. Explore the Monte Carlo Casino and the surrounding area.
- **Evening**: Return to Menton. Have dinner at a restaurant of your choice.

## Day 7: Scenic Drive and Towns

- **Morning**: Rent a car and embark on a scenic drive along the French Riviera. Visit picturesque towns like Eze and Villefranche-sur-Mer.
- **Afternoon**: Lunch in one of the towns. Continue exploring the scenic routes and charming villages.
- **Evening**: Return to Menton. Dinner at a local restaurant and enjoy a quiet evening.

## Day 8: Exploring Italian Border Towns

- **Morning**: Take a day trip to the Italian border town of Ventimiglia. Visit the local markets and explore the town's attractions.

- **Afternoon**: Lunch in Ventimiglia. Explore the nearby beaches or enjoy the town's cafes.
- **Evening**: Return to Menton. Enjoy a relaxed dinner at a restaurant.

## Day 9: Local Markets and Shopping

- **Morning**: Visit the Menton Market for local produce and souvenirs. Explore the shops in the Old Town.
- **Afternoon**: Lunch at a nearby café. Continue shopping or visit any remaining attractions.
- **Evening**: Have a final dinner at a favorite restaurant. Enjoy a leisurely evening walk through the town.

## Day 10: Departure

- **Morning**: Check out of your accommodation. Depending on your departure time, you may have a final stroll or meal in Menton.
- **Afternoon**: Travel back to Nice Côte d'Azur Airport. Prepare for your departure.

# Chapter 6

## *Day Trips and Excursions*

**Exploring Nearby Villages**

Menton's strategic location on the French Riviera offers convenient access to several charming nearby villages that make for excellent day trips. Each village has its own unique character and attractions, providing visitors with a rich experience beyond Menton itself.

**Roquebrune-Cap-Martin** is one such village, located just a short drive from Menton. This picturesque village is renowned for its medieval architecture and stunning coastal views. The village is situated on a rocky promontory overlooking the Mediterranean Sea, offering spectacular vistas. A visit to Roquebrune-Cap-Martin would be incomplete without exploring its historic castle, which dates back to the 10th century. The castle offers panoramic views of the surrounding area and the coastline. The entry to the castle is free, but guided tours are available for a fee of approximately €10 per person. +33 (0)4 93 28 17 30.

Another delightful village to explore is **Gorbio**, located about 12 kilometers from Menton. Gorbio is known for its well-preserved medieval streets and charming stone houses. The village is also home to the Church of Saint-Martin, a historic church with beautiful frescoes and an ancient bell tower. Gorbio is a great destination for a leisurely stroll through its narrow, winding streets and enjoying its serene atmosphere. The village hosts a local market on Saturdays where visitors can purchase fresh produce and artisanal goods. Entry to the church and the market is free, but small fees may apply for special events. For more information, visit the https://www.gorbio.fr or call +33 (0)4 93 35 43 91.

Èze is another nearby village worth visiting. Located about 10 kilometers from Menton, Èze is perched on a hilltop and offers breathtaking views of the Mediterranean Sea. The village is famous for its narrow, cobblestone streets and the exotic garden located at the top of the hill. The Jardin Exotique d'Èze features a diverse collection of cacti and succulents and provides panoramic views of the coastline. The entrance fee for the garden is approximately €6 per person. For more information, visit https://www.eze-tourisme.com or call +33 (0)4 93 41 26 83.

Each of these villages is easily accessible from Menton by car or public transport, making them ideal for a day trip. Renting a car or using local bus services are convenient options for reaching these destinations. Be sure to check local transport schedules and availability before planning your trip.

## Visits to Monaco and Italian Border Towns

A visit to **Monaco** is a must for those staying in Menton. Located just 10 kilometers away, Monaco is a sovereign city-state renowned for its luxury and glamour. Key attractions in Monaco include the **Monte Carlo Casino**, the **Prince's Palace**, and the **Oceanographic Museum**. The Monte Carlo Casino, located at Place du Casino, is an iconic landmark known for its opulent architecture and gaming facilities. Entrance to the casino is free, but there is a dress code and age restriction for entry. For more details, visit https://www.casinomontecarlo.com or call +377 98 06 21 21.

The Prince's Palace, situated on Monaco's highest point, offers a glimpse into the royal family's history and daily life. The palace is open to visitors from April to October, with an entry fee of approximately €10 per person. For more information, visit https://www.palais.mc or call +377 93 25 18 31.

The Oceanographic Museum, located at 17 Avenue Saint-Martin, is dedicated to marine science and features an extensive collection of marine life exhibits. The museum is open daily, with an entry fee of about €14 per person. For more details, visit https://www.oceano.mc or call +377 93 15 36 00.

For those interested in exploring Italian border towns, **Ventimiglia** is a popular choice. Located just across the border from Menton, Ventimiglia is known for its vibrant market, which operates every Friday. The market offers a variety of goods, including fresh produce, clothing, and local products. Additionally, Ventimiglia has a charming old town with narrow streets and historic buildings. The market is free to enter, but purchases will incur additional costs. For more information, visit https://www.ventimiglia.it or call +39 0184 355 313.

**San Remo**, another Italian town located about 30 kilometers from Menton, is known for its beautiful coastal promenade and vibrant cultural scene. The town is famous for the San Remo

Music Festival, held annually in February, which attracts music lovers from around the world. San Remo also offers numerous shopping and dining opportunities along its main street, Via Matteotti. +39 0184 586 111.

Traveling to these destinations from Menton is straightforward, with options including driving, train travel, or organized tours. Be sure to check transportation schedules and availability to ensure a smooth and enjoyable trip.

**Scenic Drives and Tours**

For those who enjoy exploring at their own pace, scenic drives and tours around Menton offer a chance to experience the stunning landscapes of the French Riviera and the surrounding areas. One notable route is the **Corniche Inférieure**, also known as the Lower Corniche Road. This scenic drive follows the coastline from Menton to Nice, offering breathtaking views of the Mediterranean Sea and picturesque coastal towns. Along the way, drivers can enjoy stops at charming villages such as Villefranche-sur-Mer and Beaulieu-sur-Mer.

The **Route des Grandes Alpes** is another scenic drive that begins in Menton and extends through the French Alps to Lake Geneva. This route offers spectacular mountain views and passes through several charming Alpine villages. It is a longer drive, so it is recommended for those with more time to explore.

For a more organized experience, consider joining a guided tour of the French Riviera. Various tour operators offer excursions that include visits to Monaco, Cannes, Nice, and other notable destinations along the coast. These tours often include transportation, guided commentary, and visits to key attractions, providing a comprehensive overview of the region.

One reputable tour operator is **French Riviera Tours**, which offers a range of day trips and excursions from Menton. +33 (0)4 93 87 10 90.

Another option is **Côte d'Azur Travel**, which provides customized tours and transportation services throughout the French Riviera. +33 (0)4 93 92 12 50.

# Chapter 7

## *Practical Information*

### Travel Tips and Safety

When traveling to Menton, it is essential to be well-prepared to ensure a smooth and enjoyable experience. Adhering to some practical travel tips and understanding local safety considerations can significantly enhance your visit.

### *Travel Tips:*

1. Local Currency: The currency used in Menton, like the rest of France, is the Euro (€). It

is advisable to carry some cash, as not all establishments accept credit cards, particularly in smaller shops or rural areas. ATMs are widely available throughout Menton, and most international credit and debit cards are accepted.

2. Weather Considerations: Menton enjoys a Mediterranean climate with mild winters and hot, dry summers. During summer, temperatures can rise above 30°C (86°F), so it is important to stay hydrated and wear sun protection. In winter, temperatures are cooler but still mild compared to many other European destinations. Pack clothing that can be layered to accommodate changing weather conditions.

3. Local Transportation: Public transportation in Menton includes buses and trains. The local bus network is extensive, with routes connecting

various parts of the town and nearby areas. For longer journeys, the train station in Menton provides connections to other major cities and regions. It is advisable to check the schedules and routes in advance to plan your travel efficiently.

4. Health and Safety: Menton is a generally safe destination with low crime rates. However, it is always wise to exercise standard precautions, such as avoiding poorly lit areas at night and safeguarding your personal belongings. In case of a medical emergency, there are several healthcare facilities available in the town. Travelers should have travel insurance that covers medical emergencies to avoid unexpected expenses.

5. Emergency Numbers: The emergency number for police, fire, and medical services in France is 112. This number can be dialed from any phone in case of an urgent situation requiring immediate assistance. It is also useful to familiarize yourself with the location of the nearest hospital or medical center.

### *Safety Considerations:*

1. Petty Theft: While Menton is relatively safe, petty theft can occur, particularly in crowded areas or on public transportation. Keep an eye on your belongings, and be cautious when approached by strangers. Your valuables might be better protected by using a lockable bag or a money belt.

2. Local Customs: Understanding and respecting local customs and etiquette is important. For instance, when visiting religious sites, dress modestly and adhere to any guidelines provided. It is also customary to greet people with a polite "Bonjour" during the day and "Bonsoir" in the evening.

3. Travel Advisories: Before traveling, it is advisable to check any travel advisories or warnings issued by your country's government. This can provide up-to-date information on safety, health, and other important considerations.

**Currency and Budgeting**

When traveling to Menton, managing your finances effectively is crucial to ensure a comfortable and enjoyable stay. Understanding the local currency, budgeting for various expenses, and knowing where to exchange money can help you plan your trip efficiently.

## Currency:

Menton, like the rest of France, uses the Euro (€) as its currency. It is important to familiarize yourself with the current exchange rate and have a basic understanding of the local currency. As of the latest exchange rates, 1 Euro is approximately equivalent to 1.08 USD, though rates fluctuate regularly.

## Budgeting:

1. Accommodation Costs: The cost of accommodation in Menton varies depending on the type of lodging and the time of year. Hotels range from budget options at around €60-€100 per night to luxury accommodations costing upwards of €200 per night. Vacation rentals can also vary widely, with average costs ranging from €80 to €150 per night. For a more detailed breakdown of accommodation costs, refer to the sections on hotels and vacation rentals in this guide.

2. Dining Expenses: Dining in Menton can suit various budgets. A meal at a budget restaurant typically costs between €15 and €25 per person, while a mid-range restaurant might charge between €30 and €60 for a three-course meal. For more upscale dining experiences, expect to pay upwards of €70 per person. Cafés and

bakeries offer lighter fare and snacks, with prices generally ranging from €5 to €15 for a meal or coffee.

3. Transportation Costs: Local public transportation, including buses and trains, is relatively affordable. A single bus ticket typically costs around €1.50 to €2.00, while train tickets vary depending on the distance traveled. For example, a train ticket from Menton to Nice may cost approximately €7 to €10. Taxis have a starting fare of around €5, with additional charges based on distance and time.

4. Attractions and Activities: Entrance fees for attractions vary. For instance, visiting the Jardin Exotique d'Èze costs around €6, while many museums and historic sites have entry fees ranging from €5 to €15. It is advisable to check

the official websites of attractions for current pricing and any potential discounts for students, seniors, or groups.

5. Money Exchange and ATMs: Currency exchange services are available at banks, exchange bureaus, and some hotels. It is often more convenient to withdraw cash from ATMs, which are widely available in Menton. Be aware of any fees associated with international transactions or currency exchanges.

## Language and Communication

While traveling in Menton, effective communication is key to a successful and enjoyable visit. Understanding the local language, accessing language services, and managing communication needs can help you navigate your trip with ease.

## Local Language:

The official language of Menton, as part of France, is French. While many locals working in the tourism industry speak English, especially in hotels, restaurants, and major attractions, it is helpful to know some basic French phrases.

- *Bonjour (Good day/Hello)*
- *Merci (Thank you)*
- *S'il vous plaît (Please)*
- *Excusez-moi (Excuse me)*
- *Parlez-vous anglais? (Do you speak English?)*

## Language Services:

1. Translation Apps: Mobile translation apps can be a valuable tool when traveling. Apps like Google Translate offer text and voice translation services in multiple languages, including French. These apps can assist with understanding signs, menus, and basic conversations.

2. Language Schools: If you are interested in learning French or improving your language skills before or during your trip, there are language schools in Menton that offer courses for all levels. For example, the [Alliance Française Menton] offers French language courses and cultural activities. For more information, call +33 (0)4 93 35 47 65.

3. Language Guides: Carrying a pocket phrasebook or a language guide can be helpful for quick reference. These guides typically

include essential phrases and vocabulary for common situations encountered while traveling.

**Packing Checklist**

Proper packing is crucial for a comfortable and enjoyable trip to Menton. Consider the following checklist to ensure you have everything you need for your stay:

1. Clothing: Pack clothing suitable for the season and weather conditions. Light, breathable fabrics are ideal for summer, while layering options are recommended for cooler weather. Include swimwear if you plan to visit the beach and formal attire for any fine dining or special occasions.

2. Footwear: Comfortable walking shoes are essential for exploring Menton and its surrounding areas. If you plan to hike or engage in outdoor activities, pack appropriate footwear for those activities as well.

3. Travel Documents: Ensure you have your passport, travel insurance, and any necessary visas. It is also helpful to have copies of important documents stored separately from the originals.

4. Electronics: Bring any electronic devices you may need, such as a smartphone, camera, and chargers. If traveling from outside the European Union, you may need a power adapter to fit French electrical outlets.

5. Toiletries and Medications: Pack personal toiletries and any necessary medications. If you have specific medical needs, bring a sufficient supply and any related documentation.

6. Sunscreen and Sunglasses: Due to the sunny Mediterranean climate, sunscreen with high SPF and sunglasses are essential for sun protection.

7. Reusable Water Bottle: Staying hydrated is important, especially during hot weather. Your day can be kept more refreshed if you have a reusable water bottle.

## Useful Contacts and Emergency Information

Having access to useful contacts and emergency information can be invaluable during your stay in Menton. Keep the following information handy:

1. Emergency Services: The emergency number for police, fire, and medical assistance in France is 112. This number can be dialed from any phone in case of an emergency.

2. Local Hospitals and Medical Centers: For non-emergency medical issues, you can visit local healthcare facilities. Notable options in Menton include:

- Centre Hospitalier de Menton: 9 Avenue de Verdun, 06500 Menton, France. Phone: +33 (0)4 92 41 50 00/ 04 93 28 77 77. For more information, visit their (https://www.ch-menton.fr).

3. Tourist Information: For assistance with local information, directions, and recommendations, you can contact the Menton Tourist Office:

- Office de Tourisme de Menton: 1 Promenade du Soleil, 06500 Menton, France. Phone: +33 (0)4 92 41 76 00.

4. Local Police: For non-emergency police matters or inquiries, contact the local police station:

- Commissariat de Police de Menton: 22 Rue de la République, 06500 Menton, France. Phone: +33 (0)4 93 35 76 00.

5. Embassies and Consulates: If you need assistance from your home country, locate the nearest embassy or consulate. For example, the

U.S. Consulate in Nice covers the Alpes-Maritimes region. Address: 9 Rue de la Liberté, 06000 Nice, France. Phone: +33 (0)4 97 03 73 00. For more information, visit their (https://fr.usembassy.gov).

By staying informed and prepared, you can make the most of your trip to Menton and enjoy all that this beautiful destination has to offer.

# Conclusion

As you prepare for your visit to Menton, you are embarking on a journey to one of France's most charming and picturesque destinations. From its stunning gardens and historical sites to its inviting beaches and vibrant local culture, Menton offers a wealth of experiences that cater to every type of traveler.

In this guide, we have covered essential aspects of your trip, from transportation options and accommodation choices to the top attractions and local dining experiences. Understanding the practical details, such as currency, safety, and language, ensures that you can navigate your visit with ease and confidence.

Menton's unique blend of Mediterranean beauty, rich history, and warm hospitality promises a memorable experience. Even when exploring the lush gardens of Serre de la Madone, strolling through the historic Old Town, or indulging in the local cuisine, you will find that each moment in Menton is filled with discovery and delight.

As you finalize your preparations, keep in mind the practical tips and information provided to make your trip as smooth and enjoyable as possible. With thoughtful planning and a spirit of adventure, you are well-equipped to fully embrace all that Menton has to offer.

We hope that your time in Menton will be filled with wonderful experiences and lasting memories. Enjoy your journey, and may your visit to this beautiful French Riviera gem be everything you hoped for and more.

# Bonus

# 100

# "Would You

# Rather"

## Questions for a Family

## Camping Vacation

*1. Would you rather roast marshmallows over a campfire or make s'mores?*

*2. Would you rather hike a steep trail or paddle down a river?*

*3. Would you rather have a 10-minute conversation with your future self or your past self?*

*4. Would you rather have a campfire story told by a professional storyteller or make up your own?*

*5. Would you rather have a wildlife encounter with a deer or a squirrel?*

*6. Would you rather cook all your meals over the campfire or use a portable stove?*

*7. Would you rather find a hidden waterfall or a secluded beach on your camping trip?*

*8. Would you rather go stargazing with a telescope or just lay on a blanket and look up?*

*9. Would you rather go on a night hike with a guide or explore a trail during the day on your own?*

*10. Would you rather build a sandcastle at the campsite or a treehouse?*

*11. Would you rather discover a new campsite with better views or have a familiar site with great amenities?*

*12. Would you rather have a campfire sing-along or a game night under the stars?*

*13. Would you rather catch your own dinner or have a gourmet camping meal prepared for you?*

*14. Would you rather learn how to start a fire with flint or with matches?*

*15. Would you rather go on a scenic bike ride or a leisurely nature walk?*

*16. Would you rather have a rainstorm during your camping trip or extreme heat?*

*17. Would you rather try your hand at fishing or birdwatching?*

*18. Would you rather have a tent with a built-in air conditioner or a cozy, old-fashioned sleeping bag?*

*19. Would you rather tell ghost stories or listen to them?*

*20. Would you rather have a family talent show around the campfire or a trivia night?*

*21. Would you rather make a giant fort out of blankets and pillows or build a fort out of sticks and leaves?*

*22. Would you rather spend a day with no technology or a day with no campfire?*

*23. Would you rather have a surprise visit from a ranger or from a family member who lives far away?*

*24. Would you rather discover an old map to hidden treasure or a guide to local wildlife?*

*25. Would you rather go rock climbing or zip-lining near your campsite?*

*26. Would you rather have a camping trip with a view of mountains or a view of the lake?*

*27. Would you rather cook breakfast in the cold morning air or have a late breakfast in the warm sun?*

*28. Would you rather encounter a friendly squirrel or a curious raccoon?*

*29. Would you rather have a campfire pancake breakfast or a campfire pizza dinner?*

*30. Would you rather have a camping trip where you only see animals or only see plants?*

*31. Would you rather play a scavenger hunt or a board game while camping?*

*32. Would you rather learn how to identify animal tracks or how to identify different types of plants?*

*33. Would you rather go on a boat tour or a hiking tour?*

*34. Would you rather have a campsite with a mountain view or a forest view?*

*35. Would you rather have a giant camping tent for your whole family or a small, cozy one for just you?*

*36. Would you rather have a campfire storytelling session or a family karaoke night?*

*37. Would you rather find a cool rock or a unique leaf on your nature walk?*

*38. Would you rather have a luxury camping trip with lots of amenities or a rustic trip with minimal comforts?*

*39. Would you rather take a canoe trip or a fishing trip on the lake?*

*40. Would you rather see a sunrise or a sunset from your campsite?*

*41. Would you rather play a game of charades around the campfire or a game of Pictionary?*

*42. Would you rather have a camping trip where you make all your own meals or one where everything is prepared for you?*

*43. Would you rather have a campsite next to a river or next to a meadow?*

*44. Would you rather explore a cave or hike to a viewpoint?*

*45. Would you rather have a camping trip where you have to cook every meal or one where you get to eat out every night?*

*46. Would you rather make your own fishing rod or use a pre-made one?*

*47. Would you rather go on a guided nature walk or a solo exploration?*

*48. Would you rather play a game of capture the flag or hide and seek?*

*49. Would you rather have a campsite with lots of shade or lots of sun?*

*50. Would you rather cook a meal using a campfire or a portable grill?*

*51. Would you rather have a camping trip with lots of activities planned or a relaxing trip with lots of free time?*

*52. Would you rather have a family campfire dance party or a campfire sing-along?*

*53. Would you rather take a nap in a hammock or on a blanket on the ground?*

*54. Would you rather go on a wildlife safari or a bird-watching expedition?*

*55. Would you rather explore a dense forest or a wide-open prairie?*

*56. Would you rather have a surprise visit from a local wildlife expert or a campfire cooking class?*

*57. Would you rather see a shooting star or a full moon on your camping trip?*

*58. Would you rather have a campfire movie night or a night of storytelling?*

*59. Would you rather do a nature-inspired craft or play a nature-themed game?*

*60. Would you rather have a campsite with a private beach or a private forest?*

*61. Would you rather go on a mountain bike ride or a leisurely bike ride along the lake?*

*62. Would you rather be able to read minds or control thoughts?*

*63. Would you rather Be able to speak any language fluently or be able to play any sport perfectly?*

*64. Would you rather have a personal assistant or a personal chef?*

*65. Would you rather have a camping trip with lots of rain or lots of sun?*

*66. Would you rather try a new camping recipe or stick to your family's favorites?*

*67. Would you rather find a hidden lake or a secret waterfall?*

*68. Would you rather have a camping trip with lots of other families or a trip with just your own family?*

*69. Would you rather go on a nature scavenger hunt or a geocaching adventure?*

*70. Would you rather have a campfire breakfast with pancakes or a campfire dinner with burgers?*

*71. Would you rather be able to breathe underwater or fly?*

*72. Would you rather Go skydiving or bungee jumping?*

*73. Would you rather go on a kayak adventure or a paddleboard excursion?*

*74. Would you rather have a campsite with lots of wildlife or lots of birds?*

*75. Would you rather play a game of family charades or a round of family trivia?*

*76. Would you rather explore a swamp or a desert on your camping trip?*

*77. Would you rather make campfire popcorn or campfire s'mores?*

*78. Would you rather go on a guided hiking tour or a self-guided nature walk?*

*79. Would you rather have a campsite with a view of the sunset or a view of the sunrise?*

*80. Would you rather have a cozy family movie night in the tent or a campfire storytelling session?*

*81. Would you rather spend a day rock climbing or zip-lining?*

*82. Would you rather find a secret cave or a hidden waterfall?*

*83. Would you rather Be able to shapeshift or be invisible?*

*84. Would you rather have a camping trip with lots of physical activities or lots of relaxing time?*

*85. Would you rather play a family game of tag or hide and seek?*

*86. Would you rather have a campsite with a view of the mountains or the beach?*

*87. Would you rather go on a nature photography hike or a nature drawing walk?*

*88. Would you rather have a campfire chat or a campfire talent show?*

*89. Would you rather find a cool rock or a beautiful leaf on your hike?*

*90. Would you rather have a trip with lots of organized activities or a trip with lots of free time?*

*91. Would you rather go fishing in a river or in a lake?*

*92. Would you rather have a camping trip with lots of outdoor games or lots of quiet relaxation?*

*93. Would you rather build a giant snow fort or a sand fort?*

*94. Would you rather have a campsite near a creek or in a meadow?*

*95. Would you rather have a campfire breakfast or dinner with a view of the mountains?*

*96. Would you rather explore a forest trail or a beach trail?*

*97. Would you rather have a surprise campfire visit from a ranger or a surprise camping meal?*

*98. Would you rather take a family bike ride or a nature walk?*

*99. Would you rather Have a giant kite or a giant balloon?*

*100. Would you rather have a camping trip where everyone shares their best camping stories or everyone makes up new stories?*